Guiding Principles for Sustainable Federal Buildings

and

Associated Instructions

The Council on Environmental Quality

February 2016

Table of Contents

I. Purpose

In 2006, Federal agencies owning and operating more than 90% of all Federal facilities signed the *Memorandum of Understanding for Federal Leadership in High Performance and Sustainable Buildings* (2006 Guiding Principles).[1] The Memorandum contained the first set of Guiding Principles - overarching environmental performance goals - for new Federal buildings. The 2006 Guiding Principles addressed reducing energy and water use, conserving resources, minimizing waste, protecting indoor air quality, and requiring the use of integrated teams during the design, construction, and operation of new Federal facilities. An updated set of Guiding Principles, called "High Performance and Sustainable Buildings Guidance," December 2008, contained "Guiding Principles for Sustainable New Construction and Major Renovation" and "Guiding Principles for Sustainable Existing Buildings."[2] Previous Executive Orders (E.O.) 13423 (2006) and 13514 (2009) recognized green buildings as a key component in efforts to reduce environmental impacts, cut greenhouse gas (GHG) emissions, and lower the operating costs at Federal facilities. E.O. 13693, *Planning for Federal Sustainability in the Next Decade, March 19, 2015*, reaffirmed Federal green building efforts and called for revised Guiding Principles to reflect progress in green building design, construction, and operation practices; broaden considerations around protecting occupant health, wellness, and productivity; and address climate change risks.[3]

E.O. 13693 section 4(f) requires "…CEQ… [to] prepare and issue revised Guiding Principles for both new and existing Federal buildings…" For existing buildings, E.O. 13693 section 3(h)(ii) states that agencies will identify "…a percentage of at least 15 percent, by number or total square footage," of their "existing buildings above 5,000 gross square feet (GSF) that will, by fiscal year 2025, comply with the revised Guiding Principles for Federal Leadership in…Sustainable Buildings (Guiding Principles)…and making annual progress toward 100 percent conformance with the Guiding Principles for its building inventory." For new construction and modernization, E.O. 13693 recommits the Federal Government to these revised Guiding Principles, and beginning in fiscal year (FY) 2020, to design new buildings to be net-zero energy by FY 2030. The June 10, 2015 Implementing Instructions to E.O. 13693 confirmed that agencies "…shall ensure that all new major construction [and] renovation…of buildings over 5,000 gross square feet compl[y]with the Guiding Principles where cost-effective."[4] E.O. 13693 reconfirmed that green building work is an important part of Federal efforts to protect the environment, support communities, and address climate change.

This document updates and replaces the December 2008 Guiding Principles to:

1) Reflect the evolution of sustainable building design, construction, and operating practices since 2008,
2) Incorporate other building-related E.O. 13693 requirements,
3) Increase the economic and environmental benefits of Federal investments in facilities,
4) Enhance occupant health, wellness, and productivity,

---

[1] www.fedcenter.gov/_kd/Items/actions.cfm?action=Show&item_id=4713&destination=ShowItem
[2] www.wbdg.org/pdfs/hpsb_guidance.pdf
[3] www.gpo.gov/fdsys/pkg/FR-2015-03-25/pdf/2015-07016.pdf
[4] www.whitehouse.gov/sites/default/files/docs/eo_13693_implementing_instructions_june_10_2015.pdf

5) Include climate resilience in building design, construction, and operations, and protect Federal facilities investments from the potential impacts of climate change, and

6) Provide information on tracking agency green building performance.

II. Applicability

The Guiding Principles for new construction and modernization apply to all new Federally owned buildings over 5,000 square feet. The Guiding Principles for existing buildings should be adopted for agencies' existing portfolio of Federally owned buildings over 5,000 square feet. Agencies must ensure that they meet the Guiding Principles on at least 15% of these existing buildings (either by building or by square footage) no later than FY 2025. Once an agency achieves 15% compliance, it should set annual targets and continue to strive to apply the guiding principles to 100% of its building inventory. The Guiding Principles do not apply to those buildings where a Report of Excess (ROE) has been submitted to GSA, a Determination of Disposal has been made, or the building has been classified as Surplus. Agencies should check the Annual Federal Real Property Profile Guidance for additional details. For facilities located outside of the United States, consider the provisions of Section 17 of E.O. 13693 to determine applicability of the Guiding Principles.

Leases will no longer be included in calculating compliance with the Guiding Principles. However, agencies should strive to incorporate as many of the Guiding Principles as possible in new lease actions.

When evaluating compliance with the Guiding Principles, the new construction and modernization criteria should be applied for all new construction and when the project that an agency is undertaking in an existing building is essentially a comprehensive replacement or restoration of virtually all major systems, interior work (such as ceilings, partitions, doors, floor finishes, etc.), and building elements and features.

The Guiding Principles apply to buildings, as well as some functions inherent in optimizing building utilization, including integrated design and operation and maintenance. Some of these concepts, such as occupant health and wellness, overlap with multiple principles. Occupant health and wellness represents a new focus area not included in the 2008 Guiding Principles and so it is highlighted as its own new principle below, despite overlap with other principles such as integrated design and indoor environmental quality. Examples of occupant health and wellness areas that overlap with multiple principles include indoor air quality, accessibility of staircases, fitness facilities, bicycle commuter facilities, and healthy dining options. Similarly, climate resilience and adaptation, which is new and therefore has a principle dedicated to it, also applies to other principles.

Although E.O. 13693 revoked several previous E.O.s and Presidential memoranda that applied to Federal buildings, the following documents still apply and should continue to be used in implementing the Guiding Principles: Sustainable Locations for Federal Facilities of September 15, 2011; Sustainable Practices for Designed Landscapes of October 31, 2011, as supplemented on October 22, 2014; Federal Greenhouse Gas Accounting and Reporting Guidance [Revision 1] of June 4, 2012; and Federal Agency Implementation of Water Efficiency and Management Provisions of Executive Order 13514 of July 10, 2013.

III. Agency Determination of a Building's Compliance with the Guiding Principles

Determining a Building's Compliance with the Guiding Principles

Each agency is responsible for evaluating its buildings for compliance with the Guiding Principles. This determination should be made on a building by building basis. Each agency should ensure that sufficient evidence and documentation is readily available to demonstrate compliance with the Guiding Principles. ENERGY STAR® Portfolio Manager is one of the tools available for agencies to use to organize and keep Guiding Principles documentation; this tool was specifically developed to assist agencies with implementation, documentation, and tracking the Guiding Principles.[5]

Documentation developed to meet the requirements of consensus-based third-party green building rating systems can be used to document compliance with the Guiding Principles. Note, however, that green building rating systems may meet many, but not all Guiding Principles. Therefore, required elements or sub-elements of the Guiding Principles not tracked by the third party rating system must also be met.

Guiding Principles that are "Not Applicable"

Previously, there was some ambiguity in determining compliance in buildings where one or more of the guiding principles, elements, or sub-elements were not applicable to the building under evaluation. For building evaluation purposes, "not applicable" may be used where the building's inherent function, mission, safety, or designation prevents compliance with a specific guiding principle, element, or sub-element. The use of "not applicable" should be minimized. For new construction and modernization, "not applicable" is equivalent to compliance with that guiding principle, element, or sub-element. However, for existing buildings, criteria that an agency determines to be "not applicable" do not count toward the total number of required metrics for an individual building. Agencies should document all determinations of non-applicability.

Protocols, Processes, Contracts, and Projects that May Apply to More than One Building

Individual buildings can be compliant with a guiding principle, element, or sub-element through "campus-wide" or "installation-wide" protocols, policies, contracts, or projects only where a given building is directly subject to that protocol, process, contract, or project. Examples of this approach include:

- Green cleaning requirements in a contract servicing all buildings on a campus would mean that each building serviced under that contract meets that particular requirement.
- A centralized or aggregated renewable energy project on an installation that is designated to serve a particular building or buildings on the installation can be used to qualify each of those buildings as meeting cost effective renewable and clean energy requirements.
- A stormwater management project that serves more than a single building site can benefit multiple buildings within the project boundary.

---

[5] www.energystar.gov/buildings/facility-owners-and-managers/existing-buildings/use-portfolio-manager

- Measures that protect a campus' utilities and make them more resilient can be applied to each building that benefits from those measures.

E.O. 13693 green building requirements are applied on an individual building basis to improve Federal building design, construction, and operating practices and to foster continuous improvement in building environmental performance. Thus, performance metrics such as energy use or water use cannot be applied to more than one building. Determination of compliance with the Guiding Principles cannot be determined at a campus-wide or installation-wide level.

Life Cycle Cost-Effective

Section 3 of E.O. 13693 states that the Guiding Principles should be applied where life cycle cost-effective. The term "cost-effectiveness" should include the use of benefit-cost analysis in accordance with OMB Circulars A-94 as well as A-11 Part 7 *Capital Programming Guide*.

Updating the Sustainable Building Information in the Federal Real Property Profile

Each agency is responsible for accurately updating Guiding Principles compliance data as part of the agency's annual Federal Real Property Profile (FRPP) submission. Currently, *Sustainability* is the data element that identifies whether or not a building has met the Guiding Principles. Agencies should check the most recent FRPP guidance documents, which are issued annually for specific reporting requirements.

Under E.O. 13693 Section 3 (h)(ii), the percentage of each agency's building inventory meeting the Guiding Principles will be calculated by: (1) gross square footage of subject buildings and (2) number of subject buildings. Agencies can report achievement toward the goal on the higher of the two calculations.

IV. Effective Date

The 2008 Guiding Principles for existing buildings can continue to be used to qualify buildings as meeting the Guiding Principles where agencies have already taken significant action and made substantial progress in transforming the building to meet the Guiding Principles. For existing buildings, completion of project design and/or the issuance of contracts that will result in meeting at least half of the required guiding principles, elements, and sub-elements is evidence of significant action and substantial progress. This group of existing buildings can apply the 2008 Guiding Principles to certify a building as meeting the Guiding Principles through September 30, 2017. The 2016 Guiding Principles will apply to all applicable existing buildings that have not yet crossed the significant action and substantial progress threshold, upon issuance.

The 2008 Guiding Principles for new construction and modernization requirements can be used only to qualify any new building or modernization where project design has been completed before the issuance of the 2016 Guiding Principles. The 2016 Guiding Principles for new construction and modernization requirements shall be used to qualify any new building or modernization as meeting the Guiding Principles for all new construction and modernization where a project design has not been completed.

Buildings that were determined to have met the 2008 Guiding Principles are considered to meet the Guiding Principles through FY 2025 as long as they continue to meet ongoing requirements such as Energy Independence and Security Act of 2007 (EISA) section 432 requirements including quadrennial evaluations, ongoing commissioning, benchmarking, and operating and maintenance requirements. Also, for these [grandfathered] buildings, agencies should add the sixth Guiding Principle on Resilience as they implement the ongoing requirements for a four-year evaluation.

Likewise, buildings that have been determined to meet the 2016 Guiding Principles for new construction and modernization can be considered as meeting the Guiding Principles if they continue to meet ongoing sustainable operating requirements such as recommissioning every four years, benchmarking, waste diversion, etc.

V. General Provisions

The revised Guiding Principles shall be implemented consistent with applicable law and regulations, and subject to the availability of appropriations or other authorized funding. The revised Guiding Principles do not supersede or invalidate any existing laws, regulations, or other legal requirements. If there is any conflict between the revised Guiding Principles, and a statute, regulation, or executive order, the statute, regulation, or executive order governs. This document is intended solely to improve the internal management of the Executive Branch. It is not intended to, and does not, create any right or benefit, substantive or procedural, enforceable by any party against the United States, its departments, agencies, or entities, its officers, employees, or agents, or any other person.

VI. Guiding Principles for Sustainable Buildings

A. Guiding Principles for New Construction and Modernization

1. Employ Integrated Design Principles

a. Sustainable Locations

Consider the environmental impact of siting decisions when making new facility investments and balance those concerns with cost and security. The guidance included in Implementing Instructions-Sustainable Locations for Federal Facilities highlights the need to strike the appropriate balance.[6] Consider site-specific long-term climate change impacts such as drought, flood, wind, and wildfire risks. Prioritize sites that offer robust transportation options, including walking, biking, and transit, and minimize the combined greenhouse gas emissions of the building and associated commuter and visitor transportation emissions over the project's life. Leverage existing infrastructure, and align, where possible, with local and regional planning goals; protect natural, historic, and cultural resources.

---

[6] Implementing Instructions-Sustainable Locations for Federal Facilities:
www.whitehouse.gov/sites/default/files/microsites/ceq/implementing_instructions_-_sustainable_locations_for_federal_facilities_9152011.pdf

b. Integrated Design

Use a collaborative, integrated process and team to plan, program, design, construct, commission, and transition to operation each new building project or modernization. Ensure that the process and team:

    i.   Integrate the use of OMB's Circular A-11, Part 7, *Capital Programming Guide*.

   ii.   Establish performance goals for energy, water, materials, indoor environmental quality, and daylighting along with other comprehensive design goals and ensure incorporation of these goals throughout the design and life cycle of the building.

  iii.   Follow sustainable landscape design principles[7] including protection and promotion of pollinator habitat.[8,9]

  iv.   Evaluate and provide appropriate electric vehicle charging infrastructure, in accordance with applicable laws and regulations.

   v.   Consider design choices that improve environmental performance, protect historic properties, enhance indoor environmental quality, support health and wellness of building occupants, and address climate risks, including wildfire.

  vi.   Consider all stages of the building's life cycle.

c. Commissioning

Employ commissioning tailored to the size and complexity of the building and its system components in order to optimize and verify performance of building systems. Commissioning should be led by an experienced commissioning provider who is independent of the project design and construction team and the operations team. At a minimum, commissioning should include a commissioning plan, verification of the installation and performance of systems being commissioned, and a commissioning report that confirms identified issues were appropriately addressed. Follow EISA 2007 section 432 and associated Federal Energy Management Program (FEMP) commissioning guidance.[10,11]

---

[7] Guidance for Federal Agencies on Sustainable Practices for Designed Landscapes, October 31, 2011: www.whitehouse.gov/administration/eop/ceq/sustainability/landscaping-guidance

[8] Presidential Memorandum -- Creating a Federal Strategy to Promote the Health of Honey Bees and Other Pollinators, June 20, 2014: www.whitehouse.gov/the-press-office/2014/06/20/presidential-memorandum-creating-federal-strategy-promote-health-honey-b

[9] Supporting the Health of Honey Bees and Other Pollinators, October 2014: www.whitehouse.gov/sites/default/files/docs/supporting_the_health_of_honey_bees_and_other_pollinators.pdf

[10] 42 U.S.C. § 8253(f): energy.gov/sites/prod/files/2014/07/f17/commissioning_fed_facilities.pdf

[11] Guidance for the Implementation and Follow-up of Identified Energy and Water Efficiency Measures in Covered Facilities (per 42 U.S.C. 8253(f), Use of Energy and Water Efficiency Measures in Federal Buildings), September 2012: energy.gov/sites/prod/files/2013/10/f4/eisa_project_guidance.pdf

2. Optimize Energy Performance

a. Energy Efficiency

Employ strategies that minimize energy usage. Focus on reducing energy loads before considering renewable or clean and alternative energy sources. Use energy efficient products as required by statute.[12]

b. Renewable and Clean Energy

Implement life cycle cost-effective renewable electric energy and thermal energy projects on-site. Consider long-term off-site sources of renewable power or Renewable Energy Certificates (RECs) where on-site opportunities are limited. Utilize clean and alternative energy sources where possible.[13]

c. Metering

To track and continuously optimize energy performance, install building level meters for electricity, natural gas, and steam. Install advanced meters as required by statute. Standard meters should be used when advanced meters are not appropriate.[14]

d. Benchmarking

Benchmark building performance at least annually, preferably using ENERGY STAR Portfolio Manager. Agencies should strive to benchmark unusual buildings and space types against similar facilities within their portfolios. Regularly monitor building energy performance against historic performance data and peer buildings to identify operating inefficiencies and conservation opportunities.[15]

3. Protect and Conserve Water

a. Indoor Water Use

Employ strategies that minimize water use and waste, including:

i. Water-Efficient Products

Purchase water conserving products, including WaterSense[16] and FEMP-designated products, as required by statute.

---

[12] 42 U.S.C. § 8259b and 10 C.F.R. § 436.40 *et seq.*

[13] E.O. 13693, section 3(b), (c), (d), and (e) and associated definitions in section 19

[14] 42 U.S.C. § 8253(e): energy.gov/sites/prod/files/2014/11/f19/metering_guidance.pdf

[15] 42 U.S.C. § 8253(f) (8): energy.gov/sites/prod/files/2014/09/f18/benchmarking_guidance08-2014.pdf

[16] www3.epa.gov/watersense/

ii. Water Meters

Install building level water meters to allow for the management of water use during occupancy, including detection of leaks.

iii. Cooling Towers

Optimize cooling tower operations.

iv. Single Pass Cooling

Eliminate single pass cooling.

b. Outdoor Water Use

Use water efficient landscapes that incorporate native, non-invasive, drought tolerant, and low maintenance plant species and employ water efficient irrigation strategies to reduce outdoor potable water consumption. Install water meters for irrigation systems serving more than 25,000 square feet of landscaping.[17]

c. Alternative Water

Implement cost effective methods to utilize alternative sources of water such as harvested rainwater, treated wastewater, air handler condensate capture, grey water, and reclaimed water, to the extent permitted under local laws and regulations.[18]

d. Stormwater Management

Employ design and construction strategies that reduce stormwater runoff and discharges of polluted water offsite to protect the natural hydrology and watershed health. For any new construction per EISA section 438,[19] use site planning, design, construction, and maintenance strategies to maintain hydrologic conditions after development, or to restore hydrologic conditions following development, to the maximum extent that is technically feasible.

4. Enhance Indoor Environmental Quality

a. Ventilation and Thermal Comfort

Provide safe and healthy ventilation and thermal comfort.

---

[17] DOE FEMP metering guidance:
www.energy.gov/eere/femp/downloads/federal-building-metering-guidance-usc-8253e-metering-energy-use
[18] Industrial, Landscape, and Agricultural Implementing Instructions, July 10, 2013:
www.whitehouse.gov/sites/default/files/water_implementing_instructions.pdf
[19] http://www.epa.gov/greeningepa/technical-guidance-implementing-stormwater-runoff-requirements-federal-projects

b. Daylighting and Lighting Controls

Maximize opportunities for daylighting in regularly occupied space, except where not appropriate because of building function, mission, or structural constraints. Maximize the use of automatic dimming controls or accessible manual lighting controls, task lighting, and appropriate shade and glare control.

c. Indoor Air Quality

Take actions to ensure optimal indoor air quality, including:

i. Radon

Test for radon in buildings and mitigate high levels.

ii. Moisture Control

Establish policy and implement a moisture control strategy to prevent building materials damage, minimize mold growth, and reduce associated health risks.

iii. Low-Emitting Materials

Use low emitting materials for building construction, modifications, maintenance, and operations. In particular, specify the following materials and products to have low pollutant emissions: composite wood products, adhesives, sealants, interior paints and finishes, solvents, carpet systems, janitorial supplies, and furnishings.

iv. Indoor Air Quality during Construction

Establish a policy and implement necessary protocols to protect indoor air quality during construction and in the finished building.

v. Environmental Smoking Control

Prohibit smoking in any form within the building and within 25 feet of all building entrances, operable windows, and building ventilation intakes.

vi. Integrated Pest Management

Use integrated pest management techniques as appropriate to minimize pesticide usage.

d. Occupant Health and Wellness

Promote opportunities for occupants to voluntarily increase physical movement such as making stairwells a desirable option for circulation, active workstations, fitness centers, and bicycle commuter facilities. Support occupant health by considering options such as providing convenient access to healthy dining options, potable water, daylight, plants, and exterior views.

5. **Reduce the Environmental Impact of Materials**

   a. **Material Content and Performance**

Procure construction materials and building supplies that have a lesser or reduced effect on human health and the environment over their life cycle when compared with competing products or services that serve the same purpose, including:

   i. **Recycled Content and Comprehensive Procurement Guidelines**

Use Resource Conservation and Recovery Act (RCRA) section 6002 compliant products that meet or exceed EPA's recycled content recommendations for building construction, modifications, operations, and maintenance.[20]

   ii. **Biobased Content**

Per section 9002 of the Farm Security and Rural Investment Act (FSRIA), for USDA-designated products, use products with the highest content level per USDA's biobased content recommendations.[21]

   iii. **Other Green Products**

Purchase products that meet Federally Recommended Specifications, Standards and Ecolabels[22] or are on the Federal Green Procurement Compilation.[23]

   iv. **Ozone Depleting Compounds and High Global Warming Potential (GWP) Chemicals**

Do not use ozone depleting compounds and high GWP chemicals where EPA's Significant New Alternative Policy (SNAP) has identified acceptable substitutes or where other environmentally preferable products are available during construction, repair, or replacement at the end of life.[24]

   b. **Waste Diversion and Materials Management**

Incorporate appropriate space, equipment, and transport accommodations for collection, storage, and staging of recyclable and, as appropriate, compostable materials in building design, construction, renovation, and operation. During construction, where markets or on-site recycling exist, divert at least 50% (by weight) of construction and demolition materials, excluding land clearing debris and material used as alternative daily cover, from landfills. Maximize reuse or recycling of building materials, products, and supplies wherever possible. Provide reuse and recycling services, including composting, for building occupants, where markets or on-site

---

[20] 42 U.S.C. 6962, EPA's Comprehensive Procurement Guidelines for Construction: www3.epa.gov/epawaste/conserve/tools/cpg/products/construction.htm
[21] 7 U.S.C. 8102, USDA's BioPreferred website: www.biopreferred.gov/BioPreferred/
[22] www2.epa.gov/greenerproducts/epas-recommendations-specifications-standards-and-ecolabels
[23] Green Procurement Compilation: sftool.gov/greenprocurement
[24] EPA SNAP website: www.epa.gov/snap

recycling exist, and divert at least 50% of non-hazardous and non-construction related materials (by weight), from landfills.

6. **Assess and Consider Climate Change Risks**

Assess potential impacts and vulnerabilities, from both acute weather events and chronic climate changes, to inform the design of new construction and modernization and facility operations to increase climate resilience, including:

a. Mission Criticality

Determine the long-term mission criticality of the physical asset and operations to be housed in the facility.

b. Floodplain Considerations

For new construction, avoid, to the extent possible, the long- and short-term adverse impacts associated with the occupancy and modification of floodplains and avoid floodplain development whenever there is a practicable alternative.[25]

c. Facility Design

For new construction, based on the most recent National Climate Assessment,[26] determine key potential climate change impacts for the project location, identify projected climate changes, where feasible, during the useful life of the building, and incorporate those projections as performance targets for project design. Consider fire-resistant design and construction to enhance resilience to the impacts of wildfires and reduce risks to the lives of occupants in the event of a wildfire. Balance options to address predicted climate change impacts against mission criticality, cost, and security to determine design parameters. At a minimum, include low and no cost resilience measures to address predicted climate conditions.

d. Facility Adaptation

For modernization, focusing on the resilience of the physical facility, take action to mitigate identified physical risks considering mission criticality, potential climate change impacts, security, and cost. Consider phased adaptation over time.

---

[25] www.gpo.gov/fdsys/pkg/FR-2015-02-04/pdf/2015-02379.pdf

[26] Use Climate Science Supplement Appendix 3 of the 2014 National Climate Assessment and the NOAA Technical Report NESDIS 142-9, January 2013 Regional Climate Trends and Scenarios for the U.S. National Climate Assessment Part 9, Climate of the Contiguous United States, or most recent.

B. Guiding Principles for Existing Buildings

1. Employ Integrated Assessment, Operation, and Management Principles

a. Integrated Assessment, Operation, and Management

Through an integrated process and team, identify and implement sustainable operations and maintenance policies that improve building environmental performance, protect natural, historic, and cultural resources, support occupant health and wellness, and improve the climate resilience of facilities and operations.

     i.   Integrate the use of OMB's Circular A-11, Part 7, *Capital Programming Guide*.

     ii.   Assess existing condition and operational procedures of the building and major building systems, adequacy of electric vehicle charging infrastructure, in accordance with applicable laws and regulations, and identify areas for improvement.

     iii.   Establish operational performance goals for energy, water, material use and recycling, and indoor environmental quality, and ensure incorporation of these goals throughout the remaining life cycle of the building and verify that they are being met.

     iv.   Incorporate goals into building management to ensure that operating decisions and tenant education are carried out with regard to integrated, sustainable building operations and maintenance.

     v.   Engage building occupants with building environmental performance information. Augment building operations and maintenance as needed using occupant feedback on work space satisfaction.

b. Commissioning

Meet the commissioning requirements of EISA 2007 section 432 and FEMP guidance.[27, 28] Employ recommissioning, tailored to the size and complexity of the building and its system components, in order to optimize and verify performance of building systems. Recommissioning should be led by an experienced commissioning agent who is independent of the facility operations team. Building recommissioning should include a commissioning plan, verification of the performance of systems being commissioned, and a commissioning report that confirms identified issues were appropriately addressed.

---

[27] 42 U.S.C. § 8253(f): energy.gov/sites/prod/files/2014/07/f17/commissioning_fed_facilities.pdf

[28] Guidance for the Implementation and Follow-up of Identified Energy and Water Efficiency Measures in Covered Facilities (per 42 U.S.C. 8253(f), Use of Energy and Water Efficiency Measures in Federal Buildings), September 2012: energy.gov/sites/prod/files/2013/10/f4/eisa_project_guidance.pdf

2. Optimize Energy Performance

a. Energy Efficiency

Seek to achieve optimal energy efficiency and measure performance on a regular basis. Focus on reducing energy loads before considering renewable or clean and alternative energy sources. Use energy efficient products as required by statute.[29]

b. Renewable and Clean Energy

Implement cost-effective renewable electric energy and thermal energy projects on-site. Consider long-term off-site sources of renewable power or RECs where on-site opportunities are limited. Utilize clean and alternative sources where possible.[30]

c. Metering

To track and continuously optimize energy performance, install building level meters for electricity, natural gas, and steam. Install advanced meters as required by statute. Standard meters should be used when advanced meters are not appropriate.[31]

d. Benchmarking

Compare building performance with energy performance benchmarks at least annually, preferably using ENERGY STAR Portfolio Manager. Agencies should strive to benchmark unusual buildings and space types against similar facilities within their portfolios. Regularly monitor building energy performance against historic performance data and peer buildings to identify operating inefficiencies and conservation opportunities.[32]

3. Protect and Conserve Water

a. Indoor Water Use

Employ strategies that measure and minimize water usage, including:

i. Water Use Evaluations

Conduct an analysis and take action to monitor facility water use and identify and implement conservation opportunities.[33]

---

[29] 42 U.S.C. § 8259b and 10 C.F.R. § 436.40 *et seq.*
[30] E.O. 13693, section 3(b), (c), (d), and (e) and associated definitions in section 19
[31] 42 U.S.C. § 8253(e): energy.gov/sites/prod/files/2014/11/f19/metering_guidance.pdf
[32] 42 U.S.C. § 8253(f) (8): energy.gov/sites/prod/files/2014/09/f18/benchmarking_guidance08-2014.pdf
[33] www.energy.gov/eere/femp/developing-water-management-plan can provide an understanding of how to develop a water use analysis

ii. Water-Efficient Products

Purchase water conserving products, including WaterSense[34] and FEMP-designated products, as required by statute.

iii. Water Meters

Install building level water meters to allow for the management of water use during occupancy, including detection of leaks.

iv. Cooling Towers

Optimize cooling tower operations.

v. Single Pass Cooling

Eliminate single pass cooling.

b. Outdoor Water Use

Use water efficient landscape and irrigation strategies to reduce outdoor potable water consumption.[35] The installation of water meters is required for irrigation systems serving more than 25,000 square feet of landscaping.[36]

c. Alternative Water

Implement cost effective methods to utilize alternative sources of water such as harvested rainwater, treated wastewater, air handler condensate capture, grey water, and reclaimed water, to the extent permitted under local laws and regulations.[37]

d. Stormwater Management

Employ strategies that reduce stormwater runoff and discharges of polluted water offsite to protect the natural hydrology and watershed health.[38]

---

[34] www3.epa.gov/watersense/
[35] Guidance for Federal Agencies on Sustainable Practices for Designed Landscapes, October 31, 2011: www.whitehouse.gov/administration/eop/ceq/sustainability/landscaping-guidance
[36] DOE FEMP metering Guidance: www.energy.gov/eere/femp/downloads/federal-building-metering-guidance-usc-8253e-metering-energy-use
[37] Implementing Instructions: Federal Agency Implementation of Water Efficiency and Management Provisions of E.O. 13514, July 10, 2013: www.whitehouse.gov/sites/default/files/water_implementing_instructions.pdf
[38] http://www.epa.gov/greeningepa/technical-guidance-implementing-stormwater-runoff-requirements-federal-projects

4. Enhance Indoor Environmental Quality

a. Ventilation and Thermal Comfort

Provide safe and healthy ventilation and thermal comfort.

b. Daylighting and Lighting Controls

Maximize opportunities for daylighting within the existing structure except where not appropriate because of building function, mission, or structural constraints. Maximize the use of automatic dimming controls or accessible manual lighting controls, task lighting where life cycle cost-effective, and appropriate shade and glare control.

c. Indoor Air Quality

Take actions to ensure optimal indoor air quality, including:

i. Radon

Test for radon in buildings and mitigate high levels.

ii. Moisture Control

Establish policy and implement a moisture control strategy to prevent building materials damage, minimize mold growth, and reduce associated health risks.

iii. Low-Emitting Materials

Use low-emitting materials for building modifications, maintenance, and operations. In particular, specify the following materials and products to have low pollutant emissions: composite wood products, adhesives, sealants, interior paints and finishes, solvents, carpet systems, janitorial supplies, and furnishings.

iv. Indoor Air Quality during Building Alterations

Establish a policy and implement necessary protocols to protect indoor air quality during renovations, repairs, and alterations, and during occupancy.

v. Environmental Smoking Control

Prohibit smoking in any form within the building and within 25 feet of all building entrances, operable windows, and building ventilation intakes.

vi. Integrated Pest Management

Use integrated pest management techniques as appropriate to minimize pesticide usage.

d. Occupant Health and Wellness

Promote opportunities for voluntary increased physical movement of building occupants such as making stairwells a desirable option for circulation, active workstations, fitness centers, and bicycle commuter facilities. Support occupant health by considering options such as providing convenient access to healthy dining options, potable water, daylight, plants, and exterior views where possible.

5. Reduce the Environmental Impact of Materials

a. Material Content and Performance

Procure products and supplies that have a lesser or reduced effect on human health and the environment over their life cycle when compared with competing products or services that serve the same purpose, including:

i. Recycled Content and Comprehensive Procurement Guidelines

Use RCRA section 6002 compliant products that meet or exceed EPA's recycled content recommendations for building construction, modifications, operations, and maintenance.[39]

ii. Biobased Content

Per section 9002 of the FSRIA, for USDA-designated products, use products with the highest content level per USDA's biobased content recommendations.[40]

iii. Other Green Products

Purchase products that meet Federally Recommended Specifications, Standards and Ecolabels[41] or are on the Federal Green Procurement Compilation.[42]

iv. Ozone Depleting Compounds and High Global Warming Potential Chemicals

Eliminate, to the maximum extent practicable, ozone depleting compounds and high GWP chemicals where EPA's SNAP has identified acceptable substitutes or where other environmentally preferable products are available.[43]

b. Waste Diversion and Materials Management

During alteration and repair projects, where markets or on-site recycling exist, divert at least 50% (by weight) of construction and demolition materials, excluding land clearing debris and

---

[39] 42 U.S.C. 6962, EPA's Comprehensive Procurement Guidelines for Construction: www3.epa.gov/epawaste/conserve/tools/cpg/products/construction.htm

[40] 7 U.S.C. 8102, USDA's BioPreferred website: http://www.biopreferred.gov/BioPreferred/

[41] www2.epa.gov/greenerproducts/epas-recommendations-specifications-standards-and-ecolabels

[42] Green Procurement Compilation: sftool.gov/greenprocurement

[43] EPA SNAP website: www.epa.gov/snap

material used as alternative daily cover, from landfills. Provide reuse and recycling services, including composting, for building occupants where markets or on-site recycling exist, and divert at least 50% of non-hazardous and non-construction related materials (by weight) from landfills. Provide salvage, reuse, and recycling services for waste generated from building operations, maintenance, repair and minor renovations, and discarded furnishings, equipment, and property.

6. Assess and Consider Climate Change Risks

Assess risks to facility and operations from both acute weather events and chronic climate changes, and implement action to increase climate resilience. Where possible, align with local and regional efforts to increase community resilience.

a. Mission Criticality

Determine the long-term mission criticality of the physical asset and the operations housed in the facility.

b. Risks from Climate Change

Assess facilities, and based on mission criticality, identify possible existing, short-term, and long-term physical and operational vulnerabilities related to potential climate impacts.[44] Consider fire-resistant operation and management to enhance resilience to the impacts of wildfires and reduce risks to the lives of occupants in the event of a wildfire.

c. Facility Adaptation

Focusing on the resilience of the physical facility, take action to mitigate identified physical risks considering mission criticality, potential climate change impacts, security, and cost.

---

[44] Use Climate Science Supplement Appendix 3 of the 2014 National Climate Assessment and the NOAA Technical Report NESDIS 142-9, January 2013 Regional Climate Trends and Scenarios for the U.S. National Climate Assessment Part 9, Climate of the Contiguous United States, or most recent.